Cat and Rat

The Legend of the Chinese Zodiac

ED YOUNG

SQUARE FISH · Henry Holt and Company · New York

AUTHOR'S NOTE

Because it is based on the lunar calendar, the Chinese New Year falls between January 21 and February 19. The calendar follows a cycle of twelve years, and the first zodiac was introduced by Emperor Huang Di almost five thousand years ago. According to legend, the animals of the zodiac were selected by the Jade Emperor of Heaven after he had invited all the animals to participate in a race. At the conclusion of the race, a year was named after each of the twelve winners.

Since then, people have looked to the zodiac to understand their personalities. It is believed that a person shares many characteristics with the animal that rules his birth year, and to a lesser extent, characteristics of the animals immediately on either side of that year.

Rat

1996, 1984, 1972, 1960,
1948, 1936, 1924, 1912, 1900

Rats are innovative and know how to use opportunities to their advantage. They love to collect and organize and tend to be most active while others are at rest. Rats need to be careful not to lose their tempers or to become greedy. Rats get along best with Dragons and Monkeys and least with Horses.

Ox (Buffalo)

1997, 1985, 1973, 1961,
1949, 1937, 1925, 1913, 1901

Ox are honest, conservative, and patient by nature. They are happy when alone. Since friends and family find them dependable, they will make good mothers or fathers. Ox can be stubborn when pushed. They may be slow in starting things, but always complete what they begin. Ox are better friends with Snakes and Roosters and can get into trouble with Goats.

Tiger

1998, 1986, 1974, 1962,
1950, 1938, 1926, 1914, 1902

Tigers are powerful, courageous, and like to take chances—qualities that make them natural leaders. Because of this, they must weigh matters before taking action on them. Tigers need to be careful not to let their brashness offend others. Dogs and Horses are friends with Tigers, but Monkeys are not.

Rabbit

1999, 1987, 1975, 1963,
1951, 1939, 1927, 1915, 1903

This is the luckiest sign of all. Rabbits are gentle, talented, gracious, and friendly. Because of these qualities, they are popular wherever they go as mediators of conflicts. Sometimes Rabbits are overly shy and sentimental, but they almost always succeed at what they do. Their best friends are Goats or Pigs. Roosters may be enemies.

Horse

2002, 1990, 1978, 1966,
1954, 1942, 1930, 1918, 1906

Horses' energy, high spirits, and optimism make them popular among friends. They have a very independent streak and like to travel alone. Horses must learn patience and learn to finish what they start. They should marry Tigers or Dogs but not Rats.

Rooster

2005, 1993, 1981, 1969,
1957, 1945, 1933, 1921, 1909

Roosters are punctual, reliable, independent, and enjoy being on center stage. They are careful and unique but sometimes conceited. Snakes and Ox are friends but Rabbits are trouble.

Dragon

2000, 1988, 1976, 1964,
1952, 1940, 1928, 1916, 1904

Dragons have a superimagination and are unique, energetic, and dramatic. Dragons are also moody and can be too perfectionistic. They make good friends with Monkeys and Rats but should beware of Dogs.

Goat

2003, 1991, 1979, 1967,
1955, 1943, 1931, 1919, 1907

Although Goats are sometimes shy, they are always loving, gentle, elegant, and creative. They must learn to be direct and to venture out of comfortable situations. Goats get along well with Pigs and Rabbits but are not as friendly with Ox.

Dog

2006, 1994, 1982, 1970,
1958, 1946, 1934, 1922, 1910

Dogs are gregarious, loyal, honest, fun-loving team players. They are also helpful and optimistic but may spend too much time worrying about things. For friendship, Dogs should look to Horses or Tigers. Watch out for Dragons.

Snake

2001, 1989, 1977, 1965,
1953, 1941, 1929, 1917, 1905

Snakes are talented and graceful, intuitive and wise. They are subtle in their ways and care about their looks. Snakes can be stingy at times, but if they use their good qualities to help others, many people will benefit. Snakes' best friends are Roosters and Ox, while their enemies are Pigs.

Monkey

2004, 1992, 1980, 1968,
1956, 1944, 1932, 1920, 1908

People pay attention to Monkeys because they are very smart. They are confident, energetic, happy, and curious. However, Monkeys can become overly confident, getting ahead of themselves and becoming confused. Monkeys should stay away from Tigers and look for Dragons or Rats as friends.

Pig

2007, 1995, 1983, 1971,
1959, 1947, 1935, 1923, 1911

Pigs are noble and physically strong and will sacrifice anything for the welfare of their family. Their friendships are long-lasting, even though they may not always be easy. Pigs can sometimes be reckless. They should stay away from other Pigs and make friends with Rabbits or Goats.

To FiFi Y. Chou,

who showed me
that bringing
one's enthusiasm
and joy of
everyday life to
the young and old
holds the key to
true fulmillment.

SQUARE
FISH

An Imprint of Macmillan

Library of Congress Cataloging-in-Publication Data
Young, Ed.
Cat and Rat : the legend of the Chinese zodiac / Ed Young.
p.   cm.
Summary: Introduces the Chinese zodiac and relates how each of its twelve signs
was named for an animal selected by the Jade Emperor.
ISBN 978-0-8050-6049-2
1. Astrology, Chinese—Juvenile literature. 2. Zodiac—Juvenile literature.
[1. Astrology, Chinese. 2. Zodiac.] I. Title.
BF1714.C5Y68 1995   133.5—dc20   94-49147

Originally published in the United States by Henry Holt and Company
First Square Fish Edition: August 2012
Square Fish logo designed by Filomena Tuosto
The artist used charcoal and pastels on Japanese rice paper
to create the illustrations for this book.
mackids.com

20 19 18 17 16 15 14

AR: 3.3 / F&P: M / LEXILE: AD430L

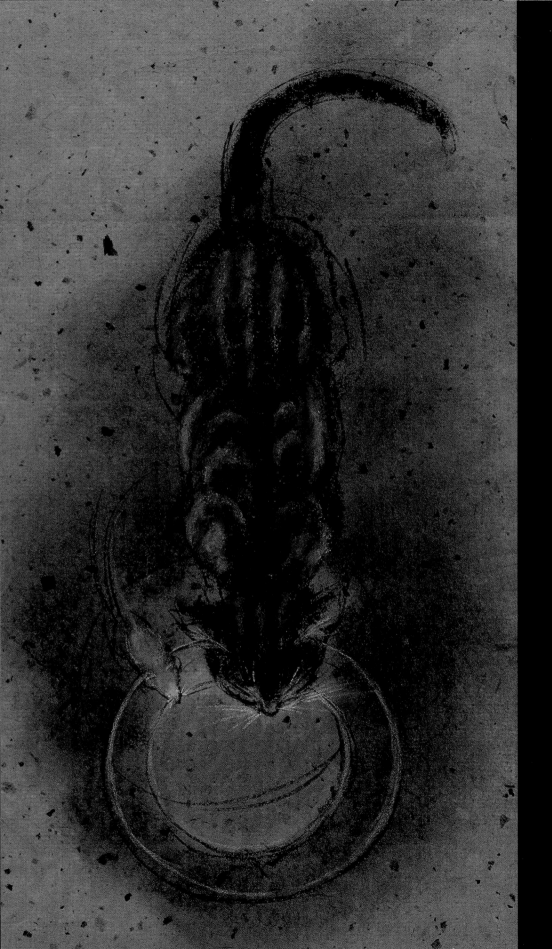

In CHINA, a long, long time ago, there lived a cat and a rat. They were best friends. They ate together. They played together. They slept together.

One day, the Emperor decided to hold a race among all the animals in the land. The first twelve animals to cross the finish line would have a year in the Chinese calendar named after them. This would be quite an honor.

"But winning the race will not be easy," warned the Emperor. "You must run through the thickest part of the forest and then swim across the river at its widest point."

Cat and Rat each wanted to be the first to cross the finish line. But they knew that they would be two of the smallest animals in the race.

"We will never make it," Rat complained to Cat.

"Oh, I think we will," replied the resourceful cat.

"We'll ask the water buffalo to help us," said the cat. "He could give us a head start. He always wakes up before sunrise. Maybe we could even ride on his back."

So Cat and Rat convinced Buffalo to wake them up early on the day of the race. The next morning, Buffalo was up long before dawn. "Wake up, lazybones," he said to the sleeping cat and rat. "We had better get started."

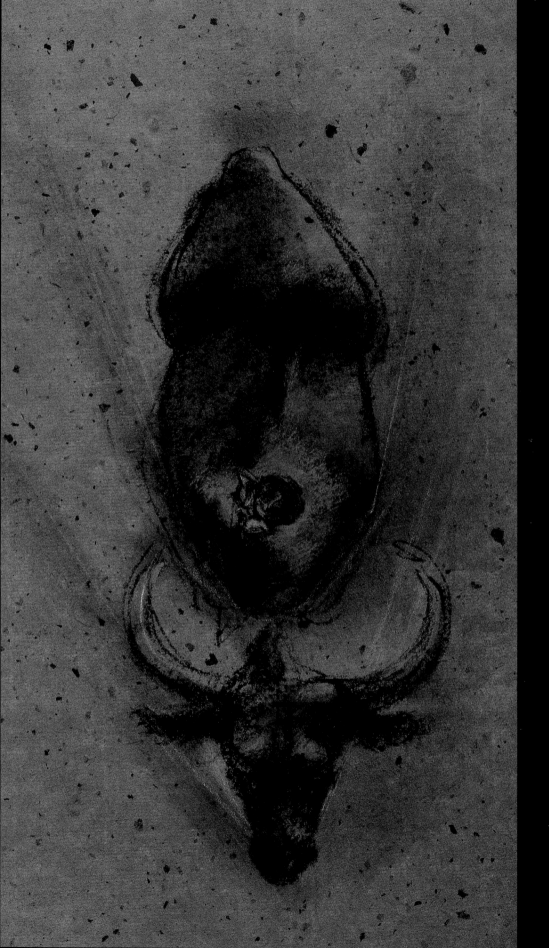

Cat and Rat climbed on the buffalo's back. But they were so sleepy that by the time they had fully awakened, they were half way across the river.

Rat woke up first. He saw the Emperor standing at the finish line far, far away. Why should I share the glory of first place with Cat and Buffalo? thought the rat selfishly.

"Wake up, my friend," he cried to Cat. "Look at all the tasty fish swimming in the water."

Cat licked her lips. She leaned over for a closer look, and Rat gave her a little push. SPLASH! She tumbled into the water.

Buffalo turned his head to see what had made the splash. He didn't see the cat, though. What he saw instead were the other animals in the race—and they were close behind him. Without giving Cat or Rat another thought, he sped toward the Emperor.

Just as Buffalo neared the riverbank, the clever rat leaped from behind his ear and crossed the finish line in first place.

"How did such a small animal win the race?" asked the Emperor in surprise.

"I may be small but I am also smart," replied the rat. He scampered up onto the winner's podium. Buffalo knew he had been tricked into second place, but he could only grunt in dismay.

Back in the river, Cat tried to swim along with the other animals. She hated water. But if she had to swim in it to win the race, she would do so.

Far ahead of her, Tiger came roaring across the finish line. "Am I first?" he growled.

"No," said the rat smugly. "You'd have to be awfully clever to beat me."

"And you'd have to get up extra early to beat me," added the buffalo.

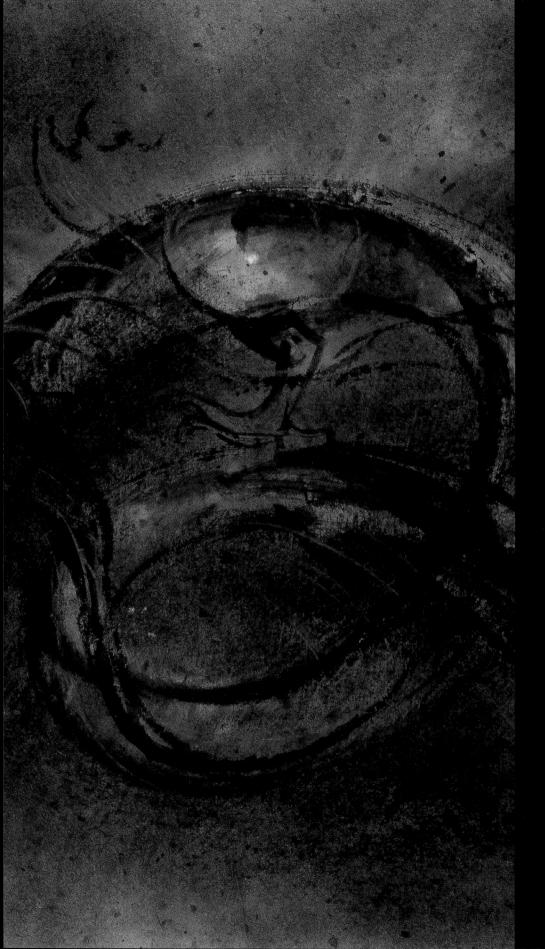

Cat scrambled onto a log.
She paused to shake herself off
and to catch her breath.

By then the sky was dark
and a great storm was blowing.
A dragon appeared in the
clouds above. He was much,
much too big to run through
woods or swim across a river,
so the Emperor had told him
he could race through the sky,
braving the rains and the
wind.

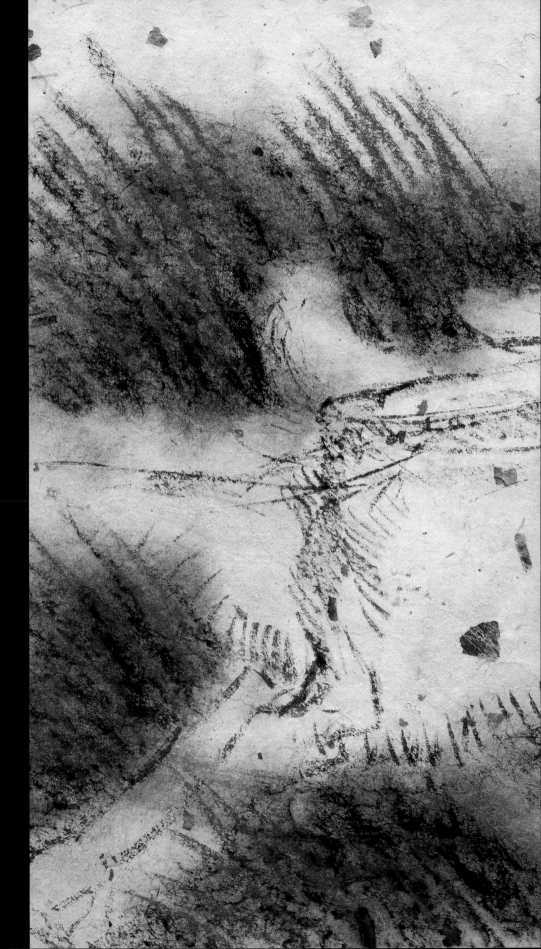

But no sooner had he begun his descent to the earth, than the rabbit darted across the finish line in front of him, taking fourth place. The dragon had to be content with fifth.

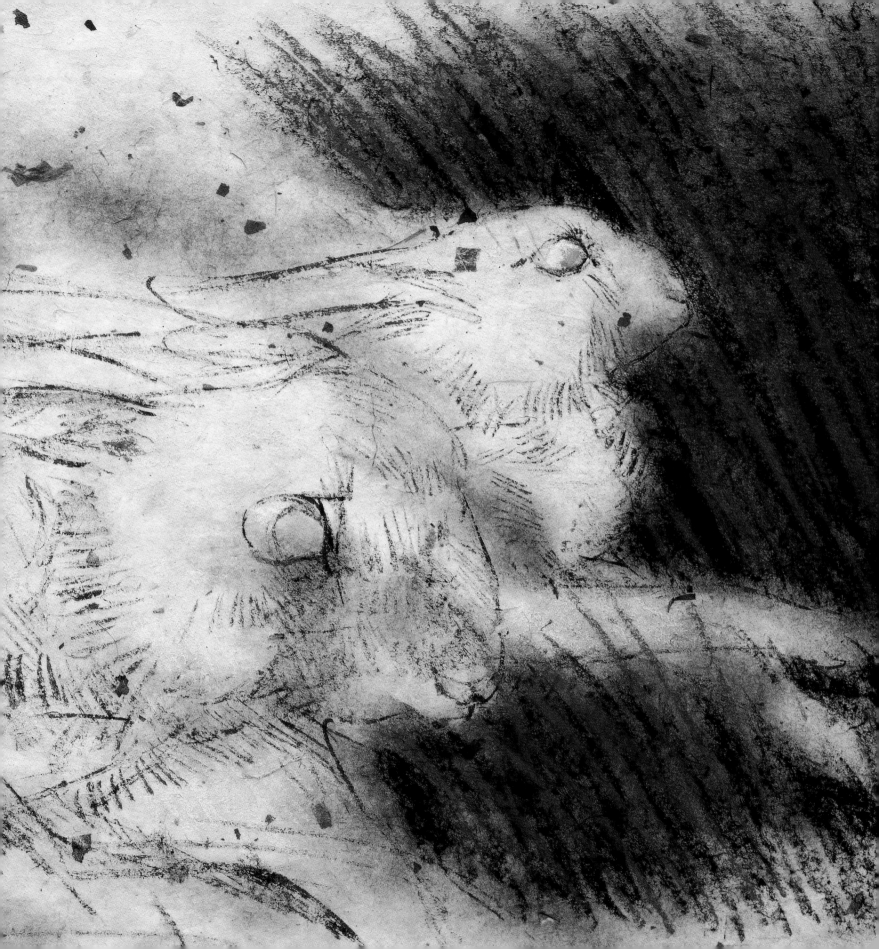

In the river, the cat heaved a great sigh, then plunged into the water again. "I can still make it," she told herself. But Snake slithered across the finish line next and hissed a silvery greeting to the five animals who had arrived before him. Snake was number six.

Cat swam as fast as she could. A few moments later, she heard the sound of galloping hooves in the distance. Horse thundered across the finish line in seventh place.

Goat and Monkey weren't far behind. They jumped onto the log on which Cat had rested and paddled across the finish line almost at the same time. But Goat beat Monkey.

While the nine winners waited patiently with the Emperor, Cat watched Rooster struggle toward the finish line. Dog could easily have swum ahead of Rooster, but she couldn't resist playing in the water for just a few minutes longer.

"Number ten!" called the Emperor as Rooster staggered in. "Number eleven!" he cried when Dog arrived.

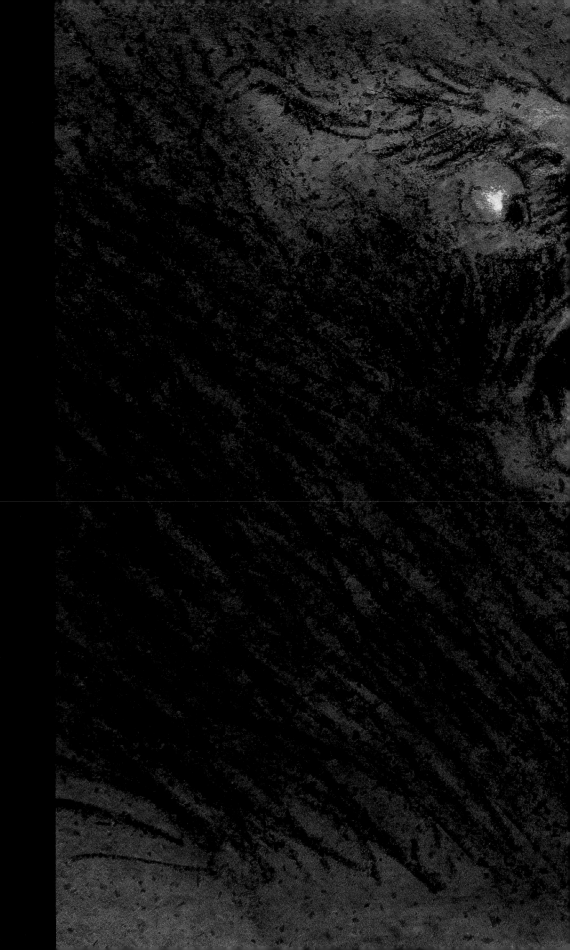

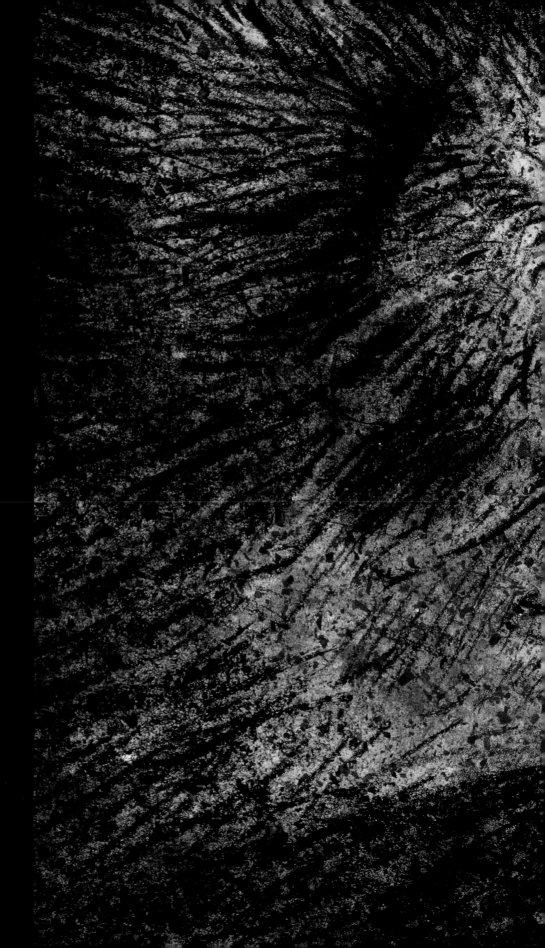

"Who will be number twelve?" asked the Emperor. "I need just one more animal."

"Me! I will!" called Cat, and she swam even faster. Unfortunately for Cat, Pig rushed across the finish line in front of her.

"Number twelve!" cried the Emperor, but Cat was still too far away.

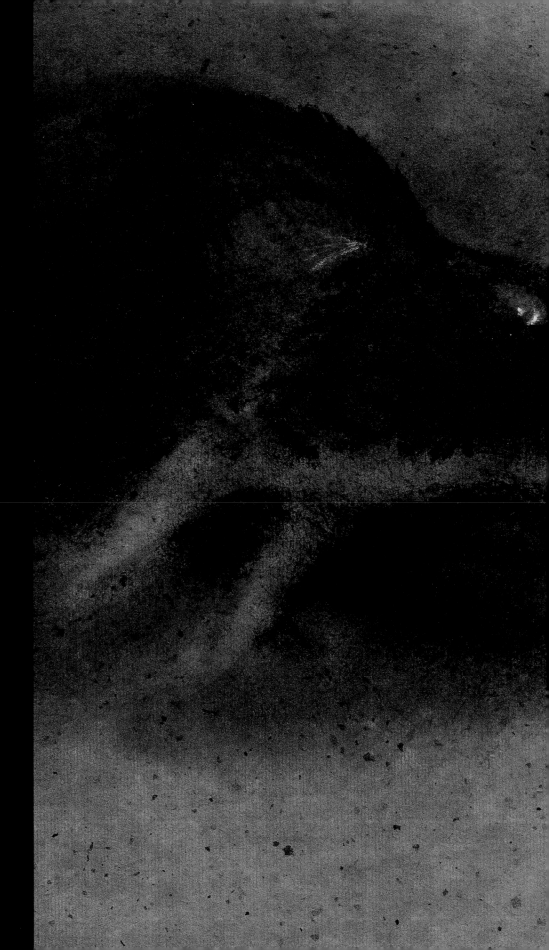

"Congratulations to all the winners!" said the Emperor. "One of the twelve years will be named after each of you."

Suddenly, up rushed Cat. She was tired and wet and more than a little unhappy about swimming across the river on her own. "How did I do?" she asked anxiously. "Am I one of the winners?"

"Sorry, dear Cat," replied the Emperor. "All twelve places have been filled."

Upon hearing this news, Cat let out a yowl and tried to pounce on Rat. Her claws scratched the tip of his tail, but Rat squeezed under the Emperor's chair just in time.

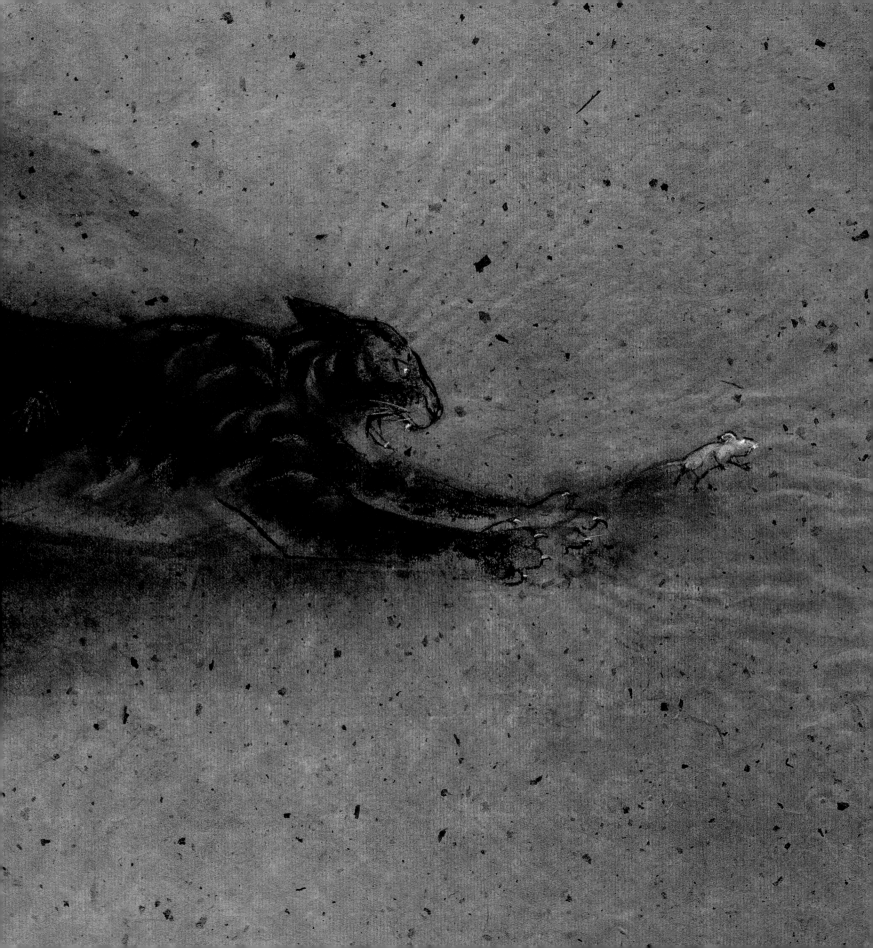

And that is why, to this very day, Cat and Rat are enemies.